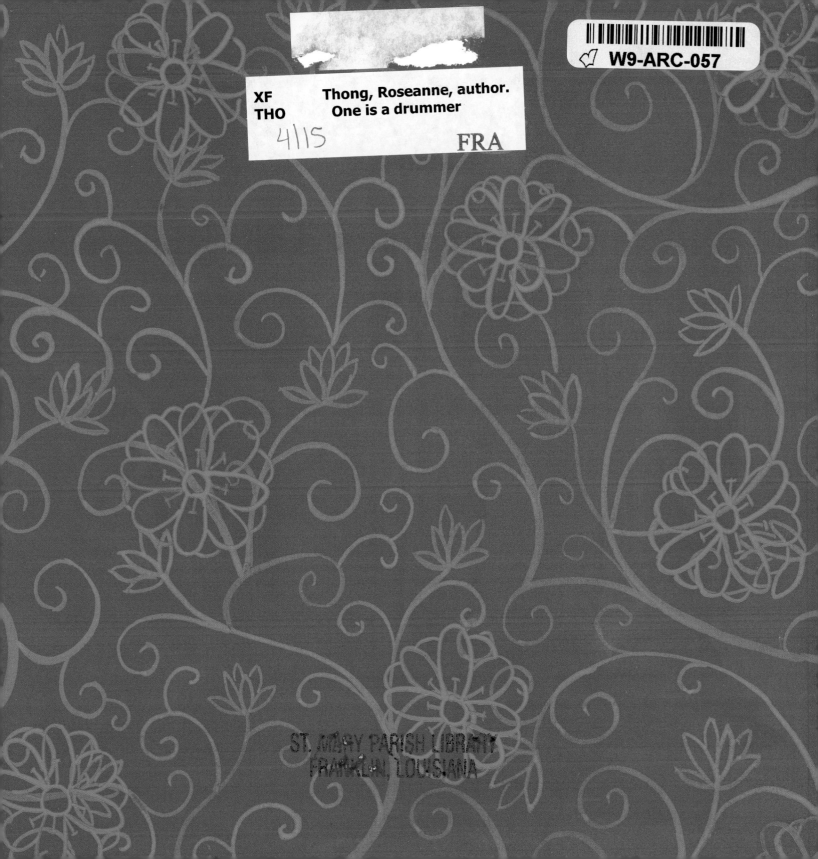

To my good friend Irene, who advised me to "just do it!" —R. T.
To Karma Lilian Kendall, who is niece number one. —G. L.

Amicus Illustrated is published by Amicus
P.O. Box 1329 Mankato, MN 56002
www.amicuspublishing.us

This library-bound edition is reprinted by arrangement with Chronicle Books LLC, 680 Second Street, San Francisco, California 94107.

First published in the United States in 2004 by Chronicle Books LLC.

Text © 2004 by Roseanne Thong.
Illustrations © 2004 by Grace Lin.

Book design by Sara Gillingham.
Typeset in Melior.
The illustrations in this book were rendered in gouache.

Library of Congress Cataloging-in-Publication Data
Thong, Roseanne.
One is a drummer : a book of numbers / by Roseanne Thong ; illustrated by Grace Lin.
pages cm. -- (Multicultural shapes and colors)
Originally published in 2004 by Chronicle Books.
Summary: A young girl numbers her discoveries in the world around her, from one dragon boat to four mahjong players to ten bamboo stalks.
ISBN 978-1-60753-567-6 (library binding)
[1. Stories in rhyme. 2. Counting. 3. Chinese Americans--Fiction.] I. Lin, Grace, illustrator. II. Title.
PZ8.3.T328On 2014
[E]--dc23
2014001001

Printed in the United States of America at
Corporate Graphics, North Mankato, Minnesota.
10 9 8 7 6 5 4 3 2 1

One Is a Drummer

A BOOK OF NUMBERS

written by Roseanne Thong ✿ illustrated by Grace Lin

One is a **drummer**
One is a race
One is a dragon boat
that wins first place!

One is a tail
   and a cool, wet nose
One is a tongue
   that tickles my toes

Two are the greetings
on our wall
"Luck" and "Fortune"
for us all

Three are the steamers
Three are the buns
Three are the egg tarts—
here they come!

Four are the friends
who play mahjong
Four are the songbirds
that chirp along

Four are the seasons
I know them all
Spring, summer,
winter and fall

Five are the fish balls
on a stick
Five are the fingers
that I lick

Six are the horses
on a merry-go-round
Six are the children
going up and down!

Seven is the number
of days in a week
What day is today?
Let's take a peek!

Eight are the napkins
Eight are the dishes
Eight are the candles
for making wishes

Eight are the Chinese
Immortals of old
Eight are the precious
gifts they hold

Nine colored swimsuits
Nine pairs of feet
Nine are the children
escaping the heat

Ten are the stalks
  of green bamboo
Ten cool stepping stones
  to walk on through

There are so many numbers
at home and at play
How many have
you counted today?

Dragon Boat Festival: During this celebration, people remember the famous poet Qu Yuan who died long ago. He is said to have leaped into a river when an evil king captured his kingdom. Fishermen tried to save Qu Yuan by beating on drums and splashing their oars to keep the water dragons away. When they realized it was too late, they scattered rice dumplings into the river so that his soul would never be hungry. A special kind of rice dumpling called *zhong-zi* is eaten to remember Qu Yuan. It is made of glutinous rice and wrapped in bamboo leaves.

Dragon Boats: Complete with ferocious heads, scales and long, thin bodies, these boats are raced during the Dragon Boat Festival. A drummer sits up front and beats out the pace, as rowers follow with their oars.

New Year Greetings: At the New Year, bright red banners carrying wishes for luck, good fortune and new beginnings are hung on the walls and doors of homes, restaurants and public places.

Dim Sum: A Cantonese term meaning "a little heart," dim sum refers to little snacks or treats that are eaten with Chinese tea for breakfast or lunch. They are often served three at a time in bamboo steamers. Some popular dim sum items include shrimp dumplings, barbecued pork buns, meatballs and egg tarts.

Mahjong: This traditional Chinese game requires four players and uses 144 rectangular tiles made of plastic or wood. The tiles come in suits of bamboo, dots, numbers, winds, flowers, dragons and directions (north, south, east, west), and make a delightful clicking noise when they are laid on the table.

Eight Immortals: These legendary beings are based on real people who lived long ago. The immortals carry Taoist symbols: a basket of flowers, a sword, castanets, a fan, a gourd, a flute, a tube drum and a lotus blossom.

Bamboo: This plant is favored by Chinese in home and temple gardens. There is a saying that people should try to grow up straight and strong, just like bamboo.